SUPERCUTE COOKIES

24 ADORABLE PATTERNS

for Icebox Cookies and Langue de Chat

YUKA ITO / efuca.

ONE PEACE BOOKS

Super Cute Cookies: 24 Adorable Designs for Icebox Cookies and Langue de Chat

Original Japanese Edition
First published in English by One Peace Books, Inc. in 2015

Egarairi de Tsukuru Icebox Cookie Doko wo Kittemo Detekuru! 24 no Kawaii Design
©2011 by Yuka ITO.
All rights reserved.
Original Japanese edition published in 2011 by KAWADE SHOBO SHINSHA. LTD.
PUBLISHERS.
English translation rights arranged with KAWADE SHOBO SHINSHA. LTD. PUBLISHERS
through Japan UNI Agency, Inc., Tokyo.

ISBN 13: 978-1-935548-95-9

Author: Yuka Ito
Photography: Wakana Baba (except for the left and center pictures on p.4 and p.79)
Art Direction: Chisa Torisawa (Sunshine Bird Graphic)
Styling: Mariko Danno
Japanese Edition Editor: Noriko Motomura (Motomura Arotea Productions)

Translated by: Glenn Anderson
Cover Design by: Tsukuru Kunii

1234546789

One Peace Books
43-32 22nd Street #204 Long Island City, NY 11101 USA
http://www.onepeacebooks.com

Printed in South Korea
1234546789

SUPER CUTE COOKIES!

CONTENTS

Introduction 04
A Note on Measurements 05
Tools 06
Coloring 08
Baking 09

1
Icebox cookies

01 Stripes 12

02 Diagonal Stripes 12

03 Crosses 12

04 Checkers 12
>>Instructions 22

05 Flowers 14
>>Instructions 24

06 Mushrooms 15
>>Instructions 25

07 Faces 16
>>Instructions 26

08 Cats 17
>>Instructions 27

09 Moons 30
>>Instructions 40

10 Raindrops & Umbrellas 31
>>Instructions 41

11 Butterflies 32
>>Instructions 42

12 Swans 33
>>Instructions 43

13 T-Shirts and Skirts 34
>>Instructions 44

14 Boots 35
>>Instructions 45

15 Cars 36
>>Instructions 46

16 Bicycles 37
>>Instructions 47

17 Medals 38
>>Instructions 48

18 Kings 39
>>Instructions 49

19 Presents 50
>>Instructions 56

20 Rings 51
>>Instructions 57

21 Candles 52
>>Instructions 58

22 Ribbons 53
>>Instructions 59

23 Babies 54
>>Instructions 60

24 Cakes 55
>>Instructions 61

How to make the dough 18
How to color the dough 19
How to form the basic shapes 20
Assembling the shapes 21

2
Langue de chat

25 Cigarette Style 66

››Instructions 73

26 Spirals 66

››Instructions 73

27 Cup Style 67

››Instructions 74

28 Cone Style 67

››Instructions 74

29 Patterns 68

››Instructions 75

30 Words 68

››Instructions 75

31 Pictures 69

››Instructions 75

How to make the dough 70
How to color the dough 71
Once you've got the dough made 72

Super Cute Ideas

Super Cute Freestyle Cookies! 28
Super Cute Wedding Party! 62
Super Cute Birthday! 76

Afterword 78
Profile 79

We use stars to rank the difficulty of the recipes in this book. Please reference them when you decide on a recipe to try!

Eggs are medium sizes, 30g whites, 20g yolks, and 50g eggs.

Baking temperatures and times will depend on your oven. The listed times and temperatures are only given as a reference. Be sure to keep an eye on your cookies when they are baking!

Chilling and Freezing times will depend on your equipment, The listed times are only given as a reference. Be sure to keep an eye on your cookies while they are in the icebox!

INTRODUCTION

The goal of this book is to introduce you to the techniques for making delightful and delicious Icebox Cookies and Langues de Chat!

Icebox Cookies are cookies that start with a base dough, which is then divided up into smaller portions and colored with either food coloring or vegetable powder, enabling the baker to create all sorts of different designs and flavors.

The dough is then formed into different shapes and chilled in the refrigerator, or icebox, to make it easier to work with—this is how they came to be known as icebox cookies.

When the dough has properly chilled and crafted into a design—using a technique similar to modeling clay—it is then sliced into cookies and baked in the oven. The moment the knife slides through your meticulously crafted design, you'll see just how much fun icebox cookies are to make!

The recipes include a variety of very specific measurements, but there is no need to worry! Even if the shapes are not perfect, or if the cookies come out a little malformed, they will still be your own unique, delicious creations. Relax and have a good time.

As for the Langues de Chat, the base dough is divided and colored, like the icebox cookies, then placed into piping bags for you to draw whatever shapes and patterns you choose. There is a freedom to making these cookies, like drawing a picture, that fills the baker with endless possibilities and joy.

Both types of cookies are meant to be fun to make, and if you enjoy yourself while making them, the final product is sure to reflect this, bringing fun and joy to the people who eat them!

I've shared 31 designs to get you started, but I hope this book will help bring your imagination to life! Soon enough you'll be creating your own delightful and delicious designs.

Happy baking!

Yuka Ito

Yuka Ito was born in Kobe, in Hyogo. After working for a number of years in candle-making, she moved to Kawasaki and opened her bakery "efuka." She moved the bakery to Tokyo in 2010, where it has enjoyed popularity ever since.

A NOTE ON MEASUREMENTS

If you really want to make delicious cookies, measurements are best done by weight as opposed to volume. Because many of these recipes require precise measurements of very small amounts, this book lists its ingredients and portion size in grams. Therefore, if you wish to have success with these recipes, I strongly recommend a digital kitchen scale that can measure accurately to the gram! These scales are easily acquired at any major kitchen supply shop, and can also be found in the kitchen section of any major retail outlet.

In the sections of this book that go over the size and shape of the small pieces of dough needed to assemble the final designs, length measurements are all in centimeters.

For the convenience of the baker, oven temperatures are given in both Fahrenheit and Celsius.

MEMO

About the Dough Amounts

In the recipes, the amounts listed for the base and colored dough are slightly more than necessary, to allow for mistakes. If you find yourself with extra dough, it can either be frozen for future use or it can be used immediately for simpler cookies (see pages 28 and 29 for examples of these).

TOOLS

Before jumping in to baking, let's take a minute to go over some of the tools that you will want to have on hand when making your cookies.

Scale

No baker should be without a scale that can measure ingredients accurately to the gram. Must be on a flat surface to give accurate readings.

Sifter

We will be using almond powder in addition to all-purpose flour, therefore a sifter with somewhat larger holes is ideal.

Bowls

The larger bowl is for making the base dough, while smaller bowls are good for dividing up the dough and coloring it.

Fork

Used for beating and separating eggs.

Large Rubber Spatula

Used for mixing ingredients and dividing the dough.

Scraper

When making a large volume of dough, a scraper makes mixing and forming much more convenient. It is also perfect for flattening out Langue de Chat.

Toothpicks

Used for adding food colorings to the doughs. They are also excellent for adding subtle design touches to sliced cookies.

Lined Cutting Board

A grided cutting board makes precise measurement easy, and is a big help when forming the dough into shapes and slicing cookies.

Baking Sheet

When lined with parchment paper, a tray is the best way to line your cookies up for both freezing and baking.

Knife

Used for both slicing cookies and as a tool to help form shapes from dough.

Plastic Wrap

Wrapping dough really helps to keep it from drying out. It also helps keep individual shapes separate and to form designs.

Zippered Storage Bags

When dough is made but can't be baked immediatly, you should wrap it in plastic wrap and store it in a zippered storage bag.

Piping Bags

Used for piping colored Langue de Chat doughs. The smaller the opening, the better.

Small Rubber Spatula

Great for working with small amounts of dough, and for transferring dough into piping bags.

Stencil

Used for forming precise circles of Langues de Chat dough. You can make these easily from sheets of thick paper.

Chopsticks

Thick chopsticks are great for rolling Langue de Chat into the desired shape.

Palette Knife

The perfect tool for manipulating just-baked Langue de Chat.

MEMO

....

Baking Sheets

If you have silicon sheets filled with glass fiber, the sheets are reusable and produce a fantastic product. A grid-patterned sheet will allow excess oil and moisture to leave the cookies, resulting in a crispy final product. In this book we use Sasa Demarle's Silpain sheet to bake icebox cookies, and the same company's Silpat sheet for baking Langue de Chat.

Silpat

Silpain

Parchment Paper

Parchment paper is absolutely necessary to bake proper cookies.

COLORING

Colorful cookies are the best. In this book we use artificial food colorings, as well as natural powders, to make the seven colors you'll find featured in these designs: artificial food coloring is used to make pink, blue, and green dough; natural powders are used to make yellow, violet, black, and brown dough. However, when making Langues de Chat, you might prefer to use artificial food coloring for the yellow and violet doughs, as this produces a more vibrant result.

Artificial Food Coloring

A variety of artificial food coloring brands are widely available at supermarket and baking supply stores. They usually come in gel, powder, or liquid types. I prefer the food coloring in gel form made by Wilton, as the colors are very bright and work well for the cookie designs in this book. Only a small amount is needed to color the dough, so the best application method is with a toothpick.

If you are using a powdered artificial food coloring, a small amount will need to be dissolved in a drop or two of water before being added to the dough.

Note: Depending on the brand and types of food coloring you use, the resulting colors may vary.

Natural Powders

Except for cocoa powder, which is available at the supermarket, the other powders may be a little harder to come by: Black cocoa powder can be found at baking supply stores, gourmet food shops, and online. The kabocha squash and purple potato powders can be found at Asian markets and online.

Note: You can always substitute artificial food coloring for these colors. Here's some more information about the natural powders used in the recipes in this book.

Black cocoa powder is produced using a different method than normal cocoa powder. This powder is jet black and retains little chocolate flavor; however, it is slightly bitter.

Kabocha squash powder is produced from dehydrated kabocha squash.

Purple potato powder is produced from dehydrated purple potatoes.

Cocoa powder is what remains of the cocoa bean after the cocoa butter has been removed. As long as the cocoa powder is unsweetened, any brand is acceptable.

Black cocoa powder   Kabocha squash powder

Purple potato powder   Cocoa powder

MEMO

What about other natural powders?

Pink dough can also be colored with powdered berries, and green dough is easily colored with powdered green tea (matcha). If you opt to use these powders instead of a food coloring gel, keep in mind that the cookies will easily burn, so its best to bake them at a slightly lower temperature than normal.

BAKING

The icebox cookies detailed in this book will be a slightly different color before and after they are baked (see below). In order to end up with the desired color when baking langues de chat, the dough should be made slightly lighter colored than what is desired, as the color will darken when the cookie is baked.

Food Coloring (Icebox Cookies)

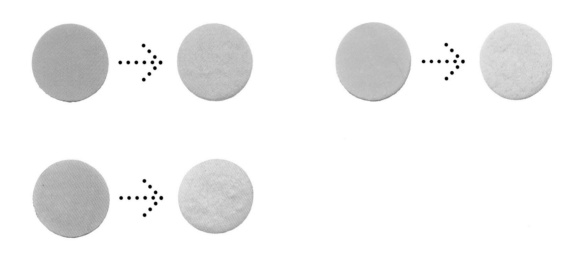

Natural Powders (Icebox Cookies)

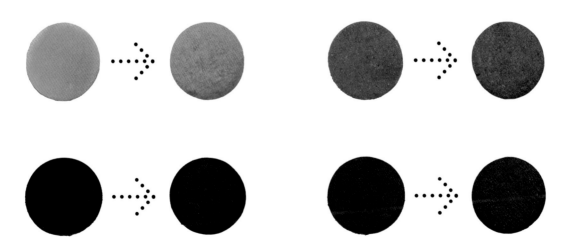

1
Icebox Cookies

HERE ARE 24 UNIQUE DESIGNS THAT CAN BE MADE FROM PLAIN DOUGH AND COMBINATIONS OF 7 DIFFERENT COLORED DOUGHS. ONCE YOU GET THE HANG OF IT, IT'S EASY. TAKE A MOMENT TO PICTURE WHAT YOU WANT TO MAKE, AND LET'S GET TO IT!

1.
Stripes

2.
Diagonal Stripes

3.
Crosses

4.
Checkers

>> Instructions: see pages 22-23

05
Flowers

★

>> Instructions: see page 24

06
Mushrooms
★

>> Instructions: see page 25

Faces

★

>> Instructions: see page 26

HOW TO MAKE THE DOUGH

I like to think of the icebox cookie recipe as having three parts: the wet ingredients (butter, sugar, egg, vanilla extract, and salt), the coloring (food coloring and natural powders), and the dry ingredients (flour and almond powder). The instructions are described in detail on this page, while they appear in a very basic format on the pages of the cookie designs. Always feel free to refer back to this page and page 19 (opposite) when making and coloring your dough.

Note: The pages with the cookie designs list the specific ingredient amounts and instruct on the portion amounts needed for the colored doughs.

MAKE SURE TO THOROUGHLY READ ALL INSTRUCTIONS FOR MAKING AND COLORING DOUGH AND CREATING THE COOKIE DESIGNS BEFORE YOU START!

Instructions

1 Wet Ingredients

(A) Put softened (room temperature) butter into a bowl and work it with a spatula until it reaches a creamy consistency.

(B) Divide the sugar into 2 equal portions and add to the butter, one after the other, working the mixture constantly until it turns white and fluffy.

(C) Separate the egg (also room temperature) into 3 equal portions and add to the mixture, one after the other, combining well.

Note: If the room is particularly warm (like in the summer), the eggs can be used straight from the refrigerator.

(D) Add the vanilla extract and salt, and combine.

(E) Divide the mixture into the number of colors and portions for your design.

2 Coloring

See page 19 (opposite) for detailed instructions. Add food coloring to the wet ingredients and natural powder to the dry ingredients.

3 Dry ingredients

(A) Combine the flour and almond powder, then sift into the wet ingredients.

(B) Combine until the dough comes together. Begin by cutting the dry ingredients into the mixture until it begins to come together, then use a folding motion to fully incorporate the dry ingredients.

Note: When working with a large amount of dough, a scraper will make the process easier.

Note: Once the dough is ready, wrap it in plastic wrap to prevent it from drying out.

HOW TO COLOR THE DOUGH

Here are the detailed instructions for adding food coloring and natural powder to the dough when reaching step 2 of the How to Make the Dough instructions (see page 18, opposite). Once you follow these instructions, refer back to page 18 and continue with step 3 to finish making the dough.

ARTIFICIAL FOOD COLORING COMBINE WITH WET INGREDIENTS

Instructions

1 Put a small amount of the food coloring gel on the tip of a toothpick.

2 Add it to the wet ingredients and combine well with a rubber spatula.

3 Continue with step 3 of the dough recipe (see page 18, opposite).

Pink dough

Blue dough

Adding more gel will produce a bluer result, as blue tends to look green.

Green dough

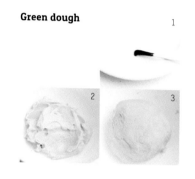

NATURAL POWDERS COMBINE WITH DRY INGREDIENTS

Instructions

1 Pick a natural powder. The amount you use will be equal to 15% of the wet ingredients.

2 Add the measured amount of powder to the dry ingredients and combine well.

3 Continue with step 3 of the dough recipe (see page 18, opposite).

Yellow dough (kabocha squash)

Violet dough (purple potato powder)

Black dough (black cocoa powder)

Brown dough (cocoa powder)

Because the black cocoa powder has little taste of its own, mix cocoa powder into the black cocoa powder in a ratio of 1:2.

MEMO

Changing the Color of the Dough

Food coloring to natural powder

If you want to take a recipe for artificially colored dough and replace it with naturally colored dough, simply increase the amount of colored powder so that it is equal to the amount of almond powder in the recipe.

Natural powder to food coloring

If you want to take a recipe for naturally colored dough and replace it with an artificially colored dough, simply increase the amount of flour used (by weight) by the same amount that you decrease the amount of powder.

HOW TO FORM THE BASIC SHAPES

When you are in the process of creating the cookie designs, there are three basic shapes that are used throughout the book: the rectangle, circle, and triangle. The methods for forming these shapes will not be detailed in the cookie designs to follow, so please refer to this page if you get lost. Still, don't worry! Give it a try, and you'll see how easy it is!

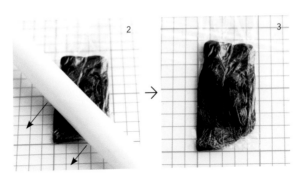

RECTANGLE

1 Roll some dough out relatively thinly and place it on top of a piece of plastic wrap. Fold the plastic wrap up around the dough on 3 sides, leaving one of the short ends open, to form the desired width of the sheet.

2-3 Roll the rectangle out toward the open end of plastic wrap.

4 Fold over the open side of plastic wrap once the sheet has reached the desired width and thickness.

Note: Using plastic wrap to roll your sheets will not only prevent loss, it will ensure the sheet is an even thickness.

CIRCLE

Using your fingertips, roll the dough back and forth until it's evenly cylindrical and the desired length.

Note: It can be sliced in half lengthwise to form a "semi-circle."

TRIANGLE

After forming the basic circle shape (left), pinch the dough with your fingertips to evenly form a triangular prism shape.

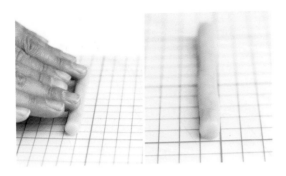
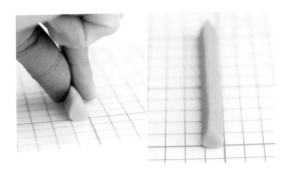

MEMO

Forming the Shapes

Pressing the various parts together and filling the gaps between them to form a larger shape of room-temperature dough makes it easier to keep the final design uniform. The gaps are best filled with room-temperature dough, as it is sticky and pliable, therefore producing the best final product.

Once you have formed the shapes, the following recipes will show you how to assemble them into a design. Once the design is formed, the dough is put into the freezer, sliced, and baked at a low temperature. More design-specific details are including in the following recipe pages.

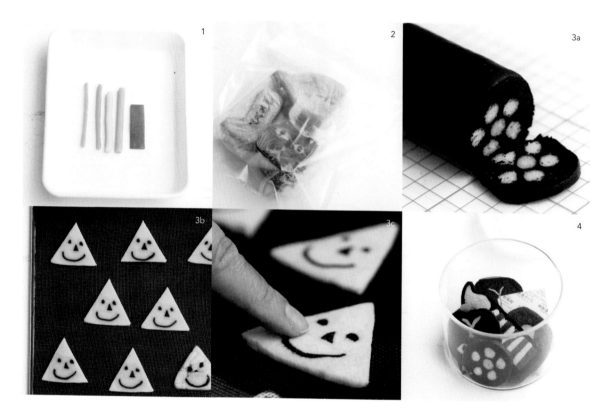

Instructions

1 Dough Temperature

Depending on the size and purpose of the shape, you'll want to keep them either frozen, chilled, or at room temperature. To freeze or chill shapes, place them on a baking sheet covered loosely with plastic wrap, and place them in the freezer or refrigerator just before use.

• For very defined shapes, like eyes and noses, the dough should be frozen solid.
• For shapes like rectangles and squares, the dough should be chilled but still soft enough that it may be sliced easily with a knife.
• Dough kept at room temperature is good for hand molding and filling in gaps.

2 Assemble the Design, then Chill the Dough

Make the required shapes from plain and colored doughs (p 18, 20) and assemble them to form the final design. Then wrap the final design in plastic wrap and chill in the freezer for 10 to 30 minutes.

Note: If you are not planning on baking the cookies immediately, the parts can be kept in separate plastic bags in the freezer for 2 weeks, or in the refrigerator for up to 4 days. Leftover dough can also be stored in the same way.

3 Slice and Bake

(A) Slice the cookies to a thickness of 5mm. If the dough is too soft, it will be difficult to get a clean slice, and if it is too hard, it will break apart. Experiment to find the best temperature.

Note: When slicing, if the dough becomes too soft, return it to the freezer for a minute to stiffen it.

(B) After the cookies are sliced, place them on a baking sheet lined with parchment paper, keeping ample space between them. Bake them in an oven preheated to between 135-150 C (275 - 300 F).

(C) The cookies are done when they have some pressure to them when touched with a fingertip.

4 Storage

Once the cookies are cooled they can be put in a container with a lid with a desiccant and stored. Note: During the summer months, the cookies are best stored in the refrigerator.

1
Stripes

Instructions
(makes 12-14 cookies)

1 Combine wet ingredients and separate into 2 equal portions.

2 Refer to colored dough instructions (right).

3 Combine dry ingredients, sift into each portion of wet ingredients, and combine.

>> Instructions: see pages 18-19

Wet Ingredients (yields 200g)

100g unsalted butter
75g sugar
25g egg (about ½ egg)
2 drops vanilla extract
2 pinches salt

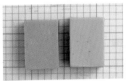

Pink Dough (200g)

Wet Ingredients (100g) plus a drop of pink coloring.

+

Dry Ingredients:
(85g) flour
(15g) almond flour

Blue Dough (200g)

Wet Ingredients (100g) plus a drop of blue coloring.

+

Dry Ingredients:
(85g) flour
(15g) almond flour

---

1 Form the Shapes

All shapes are 7cm long.
Pink dough: 1 rectangle (160g)
5x4 cm (chilled)
Blue dough: 1 rectangle (160g)
5x4 cm (chilled)

>> Instructions: see pages 20-21

2 Make the Design

Slice the rectangles lengthwise into 5 portions of equal thickness, then alternate the colors as pictured above. Cover with plastic wrap and press together to adhere stripes. Freeze for 10 minutes.

3 Slice and Bake

Carefully slice the cookies a little less than ¼" (5 mm) thick and bake in an oven preheated to 275°F (135°C) for 20 to 25 minutes.

Carve the Bow Shape

Making 2 diagonal cuts on the long sides of the cookie (before baking) will result in a bow shape.

2
Diagonal Stripes

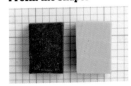

Instructions
(makes 12-14 cookies)

1 Combine wet ingredients and separate into 2 equal portions.

2 Refer to colored dough instructions (right).

3 Combine dry ingredients, sift into each portion of wet ingredients, and combine.

>> Instructions: see pages 18-19

Wet Ingredients (yields 200g)

100g unsalted butter
75g sugar
25g egg (about ½ egg)
2 drops vanilla extract
2 pinches salt

Violet Dough (200g)

Wet Ingredients (100g)

+

Dry Ingredients:
(70g) flour
(15g) almond flour
(15g) puple potato powder

Blue Dough (200g)

Wet Ingredients (100g) plus a drop of blue coloring.

+

Dry Ingredients:
(85g) flour
(15g) almond flour

---

1 Form the Shapes

All shapes are 7cm long.
Purple dough: 1 rectangle (160g)
5x4 cm (chilled)
Blue dough: 1 rectangle (160g)
5x4 cm (chilled)

>>Instructions: see pages 20-21

2 Make the Design

Using the cutting board grid as a guide, slice the rectangles diagonally into 6 portions of equal thickness and alternate the colors as pictured above. Cover with plastic wrap and press together to adhere stripes. Freeze for 10 minutes.

3 Slice and Bake

Carefully slice the cookies a little less than ¼" (5 mm) thick and bake in an oven preheated to 275°F (135°C) for 20 to 25 minutes.

3
Crosses

Instructions
(makes 12-14 cookies)

1 Combine wet ingredients and separate into 2 equal portions.

2 Refer to colored dough instructions (right).

3 Combine dry ingredients, sift into each portion of wet ingredients, and combine.

>> Instructions: see pages 18-19

Wet Ingredients (yields 200g)

100g unsalted butter
75g sugar
25g egg (about ½ egg)
2 drops vanilla extract
2 pinches salt

Brown Dough (200g)

Wet Ingredients (100g)
+
Dry Ingredients:
(70g) flour
(15g) almond flour
(15g) cocoa powder

Pink Dough (200g)

Wet Ingredients (100g)
plus a drop of pink coloring.
+
Dry Ingredients:
(85g) flour
(15g) almond flour

1 Form the Shapes

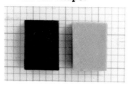

All shapes are 7cm long.
Brown dough: 1 rectangle (160g)
5x4 cm (chilled)
Pink dough: 1 rectangle (160g)
5x4 cm (chilled)

>>Instructions: see pages 20-21

2 Make the Design

Using the cutting board grid as a guide, slice the rectangles into cross shapes and alternate the colors as pictured above. Cover with plastic wrap and press together to adhere stripes. Freeze for 10 minutes.

3 Slice and Bake

Carefully slice the cookies a little less than ¼" (5 mm) thick and bake in an oven preheated to 275°F (135°C) for 20 to 25 minutes.

4
Checks

Instructions
(makes 12-14 cookies)

1 Combine wet ingredients and separate into 2 equal portions.

2 Refer to colored dough instructions (right).

3 Combine dry ingredients, sift into each portion of wet ingredients, and combine.

>> Instructions: see pages 18-19

Wet Ingredients (yields 200g)

100g unsalted butter
75g sugar
25g egg (about ½ egg)
2 drops vanilla extract
2 pinches salt

Blue Dough (200g)

Wet Ingredients (100g)
plus a drop of blue coloring.
+
Dry Ingredients:
(85 g) flour
(15g) almond flour

Brown Dough (200g)

Wet Ingredients (100g)
+
Dry Ingredients:
(70 g) flour
(15g) almond flour
(15g) cocoa powder

1 Form the Shapes

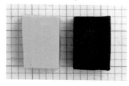

All shapes are 7 cm long.
Blue dough: 1 rectangle (160g)
5x4 cm (chilled)
Brown dough: 1 rectangle (160g)
5x4 cm (chilled)

>>Instructions: see pages 20-21

2 Make the Design

Using the cutting board grid as a guide, slice the rectangles into batons, 5 horizontally and 4 vertically, and alternate the colors as above. Cover with plastic wrap and press together to adhere stripes. Freeze for 10 minutes.

3 Slice and Bake

Carefully slice the cookies a little less than ¼" (5 mm) thick and bake in an oven preheated to 275°F (135°C) for 20 to 25 minutes.

MEMO
Rectangles

If you want the rectangles to have sharp angles, make them a little larger and slice them down to the desired size.

Instructions
(makes 12-14 cookies)

1 Combine wet ingredients and separate into 3 portions as shown to the right.

2 Refer to colored dough instructions (right).

3 Combine dry ingredients, sift into each portion of wet ingredients, and combine.

Wet Ingredients (yields 100g)

50g unsalted butter
37g sugar
13g egg (¼ egg)
2 drops vanilla extract
Pinch of salt

Yellow Dough (30g)

Wet Ingredients (15g)
+
Dry Ingredients:
(11g) flour
(2g) almond flour
(2g) kabotcha squash
powder

Plain Dough (40g)

Wet Ingredients (20g)
+
Dry Ingredients:
(17g) flour
(3g) almond flour

Black Dough (130g)

Wet Ingredients (65g)
+
Dry Ingredients:
(45g) flour
(10g) almond flour
(7g) black cocoa
powder
(3g) cocoa powder

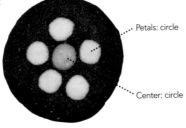

Petals: circle

Center: circle

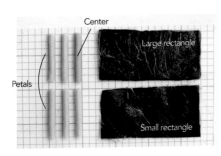

Center

Large rectangle

Petals

Small rectangle

1 Form the Shapes (all shapes are 7cm long)

Yellow dough (6g):
1 circle (frozen)

Plain dough (25g):
5 circles (5g each/frozen)

Black dough (115g):
Large rectangle 15x7 cm (90g/room temp)
Small rectangle 15x7 cm (25g/room temp)

2 Make the Center

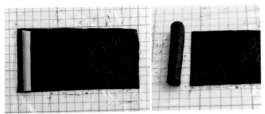

Wrap the small rectangle around the yellow circle. Once the circle is covered, slice off and save the remainder of the small rectangle.

3 Make the Petals

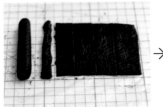 

Slice the remainder of the small rectangle widthwise into 5 equal portions, then form each portion roughly into a long cylinder.

Alternate these black cylinders with the plain dough circles (petals) around the flower center (step 2) to form the basic flower design. Freeze for 5 minutes.

4 Finish the Design

Lay the large rectangle on a piece of plastic wrap. Place the flower from step 3 near the edge of the rectangle and, using the plastic wrap, roll the rectangle around it. Once the flower is covered, slice off any remaining dough. Fix the final shape before removing the plastic wrap. Freeze for 30 minutes.

5 Slice and Bake

Carefully slice the cookies a little less than ¼" (5 mm) thick and bake in an oven preheated to 275°F (135°C) for 20 to 25 minutes.

Note: If the cookies are always sliced in the same direction, the dough may crumble. Try to slice the cookies from a different side of the design each time.

Instructions

(makes 12-14 cookies)

1 Combine wet ingredients and separate into 4 portions as shown to the right.

2 Refer to colored dough instructions (right).

3 Combine dry ingredients, sift into each portion of wet ingredients, and combine.

Wet Ingredients (yields 100g)

50g unsalted butter
37g granulated sugar
13g egg (¼ egg)
2 drops vanilla extract
Pinch of salt

Blue Dough (20g)

Wet Ingredients (10g) plus a drop of blue coloring

+

Dry Ingredients:
(8 g) flour
(2 g) almond flour

Plain Dough (20g)

Wet Ingredients (10g)

+

Dry Ingredients:
(8 g) flour
(2 g) almond flour

Pink Dough (50g)

Wet Ingredients (25g) plus a drop of pink coloring.

+

Dry Ingredients:
(22g) flour
(3g) almond flour

Violet Dough (110g)

Wet Ingredients (55g)

+

Dry Ingredients:
(39g) flour
(8g) almond flour
(8g) puple potato powder

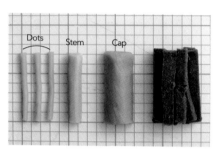

········ Dots: circle

········· Stem: circle
········· (oval shaped)

1 Form the Shapes (all shapes are 7cm long)

Blue dough (9g):
3 circles (3g each/frozen)

Plain dough (12g):
1 circle (oval shaped / frozen)

Pink dough (40g):
1 triangle (3cm sides /refrigerated)

Violet dough (90g):
Gap filler (room temp)

>>Instructions: see pages 20-21

2 Make the Cap

Cut the pink triangle into 4 pieces, and place the blue circles inside of them as the shape is reassembled. Reform the triangle shape.

3 Attach the Stem

Press the stem into the underside of the mushroom cap. Wrap in plastic wrap and mold into a mushroom shape. Freeze for 10 minutes.

Remove the plastic wrap. Use the purple dough to fill in the spaces around the stem.

4 Finish the Design

Cover the mushroom shape with the remaining violet dough and finish the design. Wrap in plastic wrap and freeze for 30 minutes.

5 Slice and Bake

Carefully slice the cookies a little less than ¼" (5 mm) thick and bake in an oven preheated to 275°F (135°C) for 20 to 25 minutes.

Instructions
(makes 12-14 cookies)

1 Combine wet ingredients and separate into 2 portions as shown to the right.

2 Refer to colored dough instructions (right).

3 Combine dry ingredients, sift into each portion of wet ingredients, and combine.

Wet Ingredients (yields 100g)

50g unsalted butter
37g sugar
13g egg (¼ egg)
2 drops vanilla extract
Pinch of salt

Black Dough (20g)

Wet Ingredients (10g)
+
Dry Ingredients:
(6g) flour
(2g) almond flour
(2g) black cocoa powder

Plain Dough (180g)

Wet Ingredients (90g)
+
Dry Ingredients:
(77g) flour
(13g) almond flour

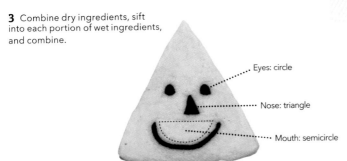

Eyes: circle

Nose: triangle

Mouth: semicircle

1 Form the Shapes (all shapes are 7cm long)

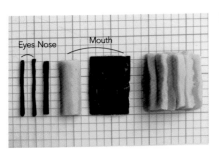

Eyes Nose   Mouth

Black dough (15g):
2 circles (2g each/ frozen)
1 triangle (3g/ frozen)
1 sheet (8g/room temp)

Plain dough (158g):
1 semicircle, 2.5 cm base (18g/frozen)
Gap filler (140g/room temp)

>>Instructions: see pages 20-21

2 Make the Mouth

 →

Wrap the black rectangle around the plain dough semicircle, discarding any excess black dough. Wrap in plastic wrap to fix the shape.

Place the sheet of plain dough (gap filler) on top of the wrap, and put the mouth on it. Return to original shape.

3 Finish the Design

 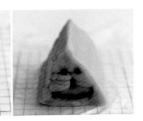

Using the plain dough and working up from the mouth, form the final shape, adding the eyes and nose when appropriate. Wrap in plastic wrap and adjust the shape. Freeze for 30 minutes.

4 Slice and Bake

Carefully slice the cookies a little less than ¼" (5 mm) thick and bake in an oven preheated to 275°F (135°C) for 20 to 25 minutes.

Instructions
(makes 18-20 cookies)

1 Combine wet ingredients and separate into 4 portions as shown to the right.

2 Refer to colored dough instructions (right).

3 Combine dry ingredients, sift into each portion of wet ingredients, and combine.

Wet Ingredients (yields 200g)

100g unsalted butter
75g sugar
25g egg (about ½ egg)
2 drops vanilla extract
2 pinches salt

Yellow Dough (40g)

Wet Ingredients (20g)
+
Dry Ingredients:
    (14g) flour
    (3g) almond flour
    (3g) kabotcha squash
        powder

Pink Dough (40g)

Wet Ingredients (20g)
plus a drop of pink coloring.
+
Dry Ingredients:
    (17g) flour
    (3g) almond flour

Plain Dough (50g)

Wet Ingredients (25g)
+
Dry Ingredients:
    (21g) flour
    (4g) almond flour

Black Dough (270g)

Wet Ingredients (135g)
+
Dry Ingredients:
    (95g) flour
    (20g) almond flour
    (14g) black cocoa
        powder
    (6g) cocoa powder

Ears: triangle
Eyes: circle
Nose: triangle
Mouth: triangle

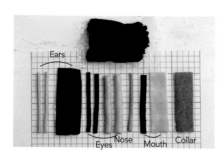

Ears
Eyes   Nose   Mouth   Collar

1 Form the Shapes (all shapes are 10cm long)

Yellow dough (3g):
1 triangle (3g/frozen)

Pink dough (13g):
1cm rectangle, 3cm (13g/room temp)

Plain dough (37g):
2 triangles (3g each/ frozen)
2 ovals (3g each/ room temp)
1 rectangle 3cm (7g/room temp)

Black dough (238g):
1 triangle (7g/frozen)
1 rectangle, 4cm (15g/room temp)
2 ovals (3g each/frozen)
gap filler (210g/room temp)

>>Instructions: see pages 20-21

2 Make the Ears

Wrap the black rectangle around the two plain dough triangles, separately, discarding any excess black dough. Freeze for 5 minutes.

3 Make the Mouth

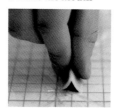

Wrap the plain dough rectangle around the black dough triangle, discarding any excess plain dough. Freeze for 5 minutes

4 Make the Eyes

Cut both plain dough circles in half, then sandwich the black dough circles between the halves. Freeze for five minutes.

5 Make the Face

Place 3 on the black sheet and work up, filling in the spaces with the nose, eyes, and ear parts.

6 Finish the Design

Once the face is completed, add the pink collar to the underside and press it into the design with your fingertips. Wrap in plastic wrap and adjust the shape. Freeze for 30 minutes.

7 Slice and Draw

Carefully slice the cookies a little less than ¼" (5 mm) thick, then use a toothpick to draw the cat's whiskers onto each cookie.

8 Bake

Bake in an oven preheated to 275°F (135°C) for 20 to 25 minutes.

Use your leftover Dough!

FREESTYLE COOKIES

If you end up with some leftover colored dough once you've made your cute cookies, you can still make all sorts of cute and colorful mosaics, messages, and shapes. You could make a triangle and then use a straw to poke holes in it: a cheesy-looking cookie! You can make anything from houses to zebras, so get creative!

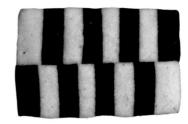

09
Moons
★ ★

>> Instructions: see page 40

10
Raindrops & Umbrellas
★ ★

>> Instructions: see page 41

11
Butterflies
★★

>> Instructions: see page 42

12
Swans
★★★
>> Instructions: see page 43

13
T-shirts & Skirts
★

>> Instructions: see page 44

>> Instructions: see page 45

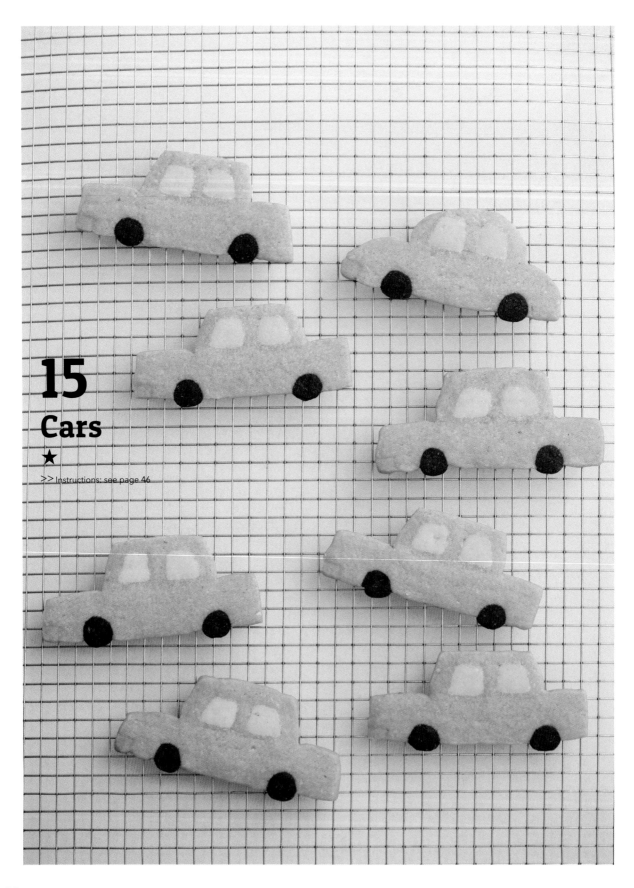

15
Cars
★

>> Instructions: see page 46

16
Bicycles
★ ★ ★

>> Instructions: see page 47

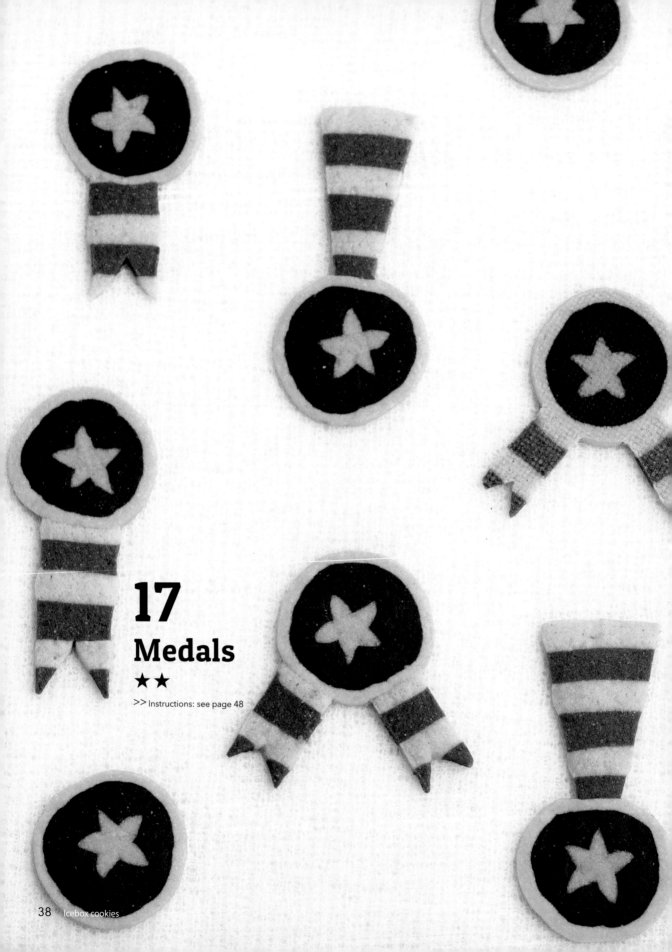

17
Medals
★ ★

>> Instructions: see page 48

18
Kings
★★★

>> Instructions: see page 49

Instructions
(makes 12–14 cookies)

1 Combine wet ingredients and separate into 2 portions as shown to the right.

2 Refer to colored dough instructions (right).

3 Combine dry ingredients, sift into each portion of wet ingredients, and combine.

Wet Ingredients (yields 200g)

100 g unsalted butter
75 g sugar
½ large egg
2 drops vanilla extract
2 pinches salt

Yellow Dough (100g)

Wet Ingredients (50g)
+
Dry Ingredients:
  (36g) flour
  (7g) almond flour
  (7g) kabotcha squash
    powder

Black Dough (300g)

Wet Ingredients (150g)
+
Dry Ingredients:
  (106g) flour
  (22g) almond flour
  (15g) black cocoa
    powder
  (7g) cocoa powder

a: circle   b: circle   c: semicircle   d: circle   e: circle

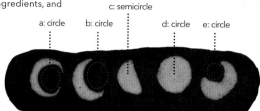

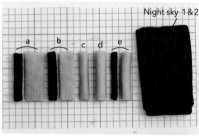

Night sky 1 & 2

1 Form the Shapes (all shapes are 7cm long)

Yellow dough (59g):
a (1 rectangle, 3cm) (10g/room temp)
b (1 rectangle, 2cm) (10g/room temp)
c (1 semicircle) (9g/frozen)
d (1 circle) (16g/frozen)
e (1 circle) (14g/room temp)

>>Instructions: see pages 20-21

Black dough (117g):
a (1 circle) (11g/frozen)
b (1 circle) (11g/frozen)
e (1 circle) (5g/frozen)

Night sky 1 (1 rectangle, 12cm)
            (60g/room temp)
Night sky 2 (2 rectangles, 12cm each)
            (45g each/ room temp)

2 Make E

Slice open the yellow circle (e), then insert the black circle (e). Adjust the shape to look like e in the picture of step 4. Freeze for 5 minutes.

3 Make A and B

Flatten the yellow rectangle (a) with your fingertips to 4 cm wide. Flatten the yellow rectangle (b) to 3 cm wide.

4 Finish the Moons

Wrap the yellow rectangles (a and b) around their corresponding black circles (a and b). Adjust the shapes like in the picture above. Freeze for 5 minutes.

5 Finish the Design

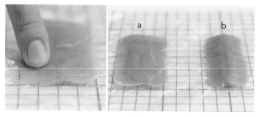

Place one night sky 2 on the wrap, and align it with part (a) from step four. Use night sky 1 to fill the gaps between the moons and form the design.

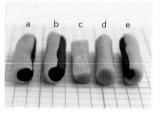

Once you flesh out the entire design with night sky 1, wrap it all in the second night sky 2, then finally wrap the entire shape in plastic wrap and apply pressure to fix the design. Freeze for 30 minutes.

6 Slice and Bake

Carefully slice the cookies a little less than ¼" (5 mm) thick and bake in an oven preheated to 275°F (135°C) for 20 to 25 minutes.

Instructions
(makes 12-14 cookies)

1 Combine wet ingredients and separate into 5 portions as shown to the right.

2 Refer to colored dough instructions (right).

3 Combine dry ingredients, sift into each portion of wet ingredients, and combine.

Wet Ingredients (yields 200g)

100 g unsalted butter
75 g sugar
½ large egg
2 drops vanilla extract
2 pinches salt

Plain Dough (30g)

Wet Ingredients (15g)
+
Dry Ingredients:
(13g) flour
(2g) almond flour

Yellow Dough (30g)

Wet Ingredients (15g)
+
Dry Ingredients:
(11g) flour
(2g) almond flour
(2g) kabotcha squash powder

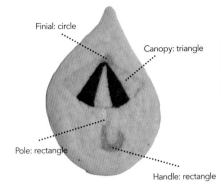

Finial: circle
Canopy: triangle
Pole: rectangle
Handle: rectangle

Brown Dough (30g)

Wet Ingredients (15g)
+
Dry Ingredients:
(11g) flour
(2g) almond flour
(2g) cocoa powder

Pink Dough (50g)

Wet Ingredients (25g)
plus a drop of pink coloring.
+
Dry Ingredients:
(21 g) flour
(4g) almond flour

Blue Dough (260g)

Wet Ingredients (130g)
plus a drop of blue coloring.
+
Dry Ingredients:
(111g) flour
(19g) almond flour

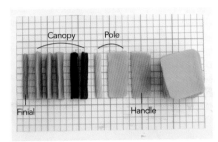

Canopy
Pole
Finial
Handle

1 Form the Shapes (all shapes are 7cm long)

Plain dough (4g):
1 rectangle, 1cm (frozen)

Yellow dough (13g):
1 circle (3g/frozen)
1 rectangle, 3cm (10g/room temp)

Brown dough (26g):
2 triangles (13g each/frozen)

Pink dough (39g):
3 triangles (13g each/frozen)

Blue dough (238g):
1 rectangle, 3cm (8g/room temp)
Gap filler (230g/room temp)

>>Instructions: see pages 20–21

2 Make the Canopy

Alternate the pink and brown triangles as pictured above. Adjust the shape. Freeze for 10 minutes.

3 Make the Handle

Fold over (1 cm) of the blue rectangle lengthwise so that the edge is rounded.

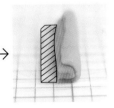

Wrap the yellow rectangle around the blue rectangle. Slice off and discard any excess blue and yellow dough to make the handle shape.

Attach the plain dough handle (lined in the pictured) to the blue dough as shown. Freeze for 10 minutes.

4 Attach the Handle

Use blue dough to fill the caps in the design around the handle.

5 Attach the Finial

Place the yellow circle on the top of the canopy, then use blue dough to fill the remaining gaps.

6 Finish the Design

Once the design is fleshed out, wrap in plastic wrap and adjust the shape. Freeze for 30 minutes.

7 Slice and Bake

Carefully slice the cookies a little less than ¼" (5 mm) thick and bake in an oven preheated to 275°F (135°C) for 20 to 25 minutes.

41

Instructions
(makes 12–14 cookies)

1 Combine wet ingredients and separate into 4 portions as shown to the right.

2 Refer to colored dough instructions (right).

3 Combine dry ingredients, sift into each portion of wet ingredients, and combine.

Wet Ingredients (yields 200g)

100g unsalted butter
75g sugar
25g egg (about ½ egg)
2 drops vanilla extract
2 pinches salt

Pink Dough (40g)

Wet Ingredients (20g) plus a drop of pink coloring.

+

Dry Ingredients:
(17g) flour
(3g) almond flour

Brown Dough (40g)

Wet Ingredients (20g)

+

Dry Ingredients:
(14g) flour
(3g) almond flour
(3g) cocoa powder

Violet Dough (140g)

Wet Ingredients (70g)

+

Dry Ingredients:
(50g) flour
(10g) almond flour
(10g) purple potato powder

Plain Dough (180g)

Wet Ingredients (90g)

+

Dry Ingredients:
(77g) flour
(13g) almond flour

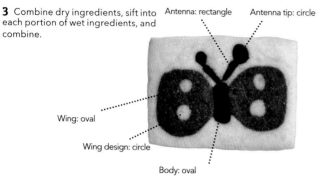

Antenna: rectangle
Antenna tip: circle
Wing: oval
Wing design: circle
Body: oval

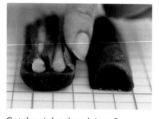

Wing pattern · Antennas · Wings · Body

1 Form the Shapes (all shapes are 7cm long)

Pink dough (12g):
4 circles (3g each/frozen)

Brown dough (23g):
1 oval, 0.5 cm(11g/frozen)
2 circles (3g each/frozen)
2 rectangles, 1cm (3g each/frozen)

Violet dough (100g):
2 ovals (50g each/room temp)

Plain dough (160g):
gap filler (room temp)

>>Instructions: see pages 20–21

2 Make the Wings

Cut the violet dough into 3 portions and form them around the pink circles as shown. Freeze for 10 minutes.

3 Attach the Body

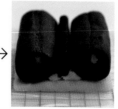

Place the brown oval between the wings to form the body. Fill the gaps with plain dough.

Lightly press the shape on to a sheet of room temperature plain dough.

4 Attach the Antennas

Fill the gaps between the wings with plain dough, and attach the antennae as shown above.

5 Finish the Design

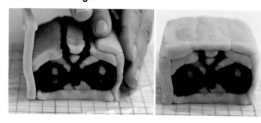

Continue filling out the design with the plain dough. When finished, wrap in plastic wrap and adjust the shape. Freeze for 30 minutes.

6 Slice and Bake

Carefully slice the cookies a little less than ¼" (5 mm) thick and bake in an oven preheated to 275°F (135°C) for 20 to 25 minutes.

Instructions
(makes 12-14 cookies)

1 Combine wet ingredients and separate into 3 portions as shown to the right.

2 Refer to colored dough instructions (right).

3 Combine dry ingredients, sift into each portion of wet ingredients, and combine.

Wet Ingredients (yields 200g)

100 g unsalted butter
75 g sugar
25g egg (about ½ egg)
2 drops vanilla extract
2 pinches salt

Yellow Dough (30g)

Wet Ingredients (15g)
+
Dry Ingredients:
(11g) flour
(2g) almond flour
(2g) kabocha squash powder

Plain Dough (70g)

Wet Ingredients (35g)
+
Dry Ingredients:
(30g) flour
(5g) almond flour

Black Dough (300g)

Wet Ingredients (150g)
+
Dry Ingredients:
(106g) flour
(22g) almond flour
(15g) black cocoa powder
(7g) cocoa powder

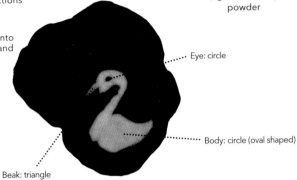

Eye: circle

Body: circle (oval shaped)

Beak: triangle

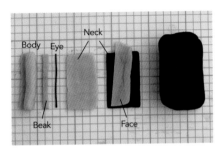

Body Eye Neck

Beak Face

1 Form the Shapes (all shapes are 7cm long)

Yellow dough (2g):
1 triangle (frozen)

Plain dough (34g):
1 circle (20g/frozen)
1 sheet, 4cm (10g/room temp)
1 sheet, 2cm (4g/room temp)

Black dough (282g):
1 thin stick (1g/frozen)
1 sheet, 5cm (11g/room temp)
gap filler (270g/room temp)

>>Instructions: see pages 20-21

2 Make the Neck

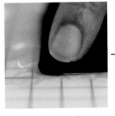

Fold over 1 cm of the black rectangle and freeze for 5 minutes.

Use the plain dough to partially wrap over the frozen section as shown.

3 Make the Face

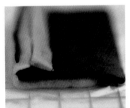

Attach the yellow beak as shown. Then attach the small black eye. With the eye in place, cover the rest of the head with plain dough to form the face.

4 Make the Body

Curve the plain dough to form the neck, then attach to a lump of plain dough to form the body. Fix the shape and freeze for 10 minutes.

5 Finish the Design

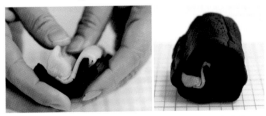

Continue filling out the design with the black dough. When finished, wrap in plastic wrap and adjust the shape. Freeze for 30 minutes.

6 Slice and Bake

Carefully slice the cookies a little less than ¼" (5 mm) thick and bake in an oven preheated to 275°F (135°C) for 20 to 25 minutes.

Instructions
(makes 18-20 cookies)

1 Combine wet ingredients and separate into 3 portions as shown to the right.

2 Refer to colored dough instructions (right).

3 Combine dry ingredients, sift into each portion of wet ingredients, and combine.

Wet Ingredients (yields 400g)

200g unsalted butter
150g sugar
50g egg (about 1 egg)
4 drops vanilla extract
4 pinches salt

Pink Dough (200g)

Wet Ingredients (100g) plus a drop of pink coloring.
+
Dry Ingredients:
(85g) flour
(15g) almond flour

Plain Dough (300g)

Wet Ingredients (150g)
+
Dry Ingredients:
(128g) flour
(22g) almond flour

Black Dough (300g)

Wet Ingredients (150g)
+
Dry Ingredients:
(106g) flour
(22g) almond flour
(15g) Black cocoa powder
(7g) cocoa powder

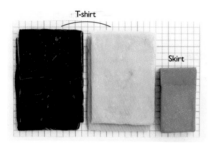

1 Form the Shapes (all shapes are 10cm long)

Pink dough (150g):
    1 rectangle, 5cm (frozen)

Plain dough (250g):
    2 sheets, 14cm (125g each/chilled)

Black dough (250g):
    2 sheets, 14cm (125g each/chilled)

>>Instructions: see pages 20-21

2 Make the T-shirt Stripes

Slice the plain and black rectangles in half widthwise, then layer the 4 plain and 4 black rectangles as pictured above. Cover with plastic wrap and press together to adhere stripes.

3 Slice and Add the Sleeves

Carefully slice the cookies a little less than ¼" (5 mm) thick.

To create the sleeves, slice 3/8" (1 cm) off each side of each cookie lengthwise. To attach the sleeves, make a diagonal slice at the top of each sleeve and use your fingertips to adhere them to the shirt.

4 Attach the Skirt

To make the shirt a V-neck, make 2 diagonal slices into the neckline. Use your fingertips to adhere the skirt to the bottom of the shirt, then make a diagonal slice on each side of the skirt to give it a more triangular shape.

5 Bake

Bake in an oven preheated to 275°F (135°C) for 20 to 25 minutes.

Instructions
(makes 12-14 cookies)

1 Combine wet ingredients and separate into 3 portions as shown to the right.

2 Refer to colored dough instructions (right).

3 Combine dry ingredients, sift into each portion of wet ingredients, and combine.

Wet Ingredients (yields 100g)

50g unsalted butter
37g granulated sugar
13g egg (about ¼ egg)
2 drops vanilla extract
Pinch of salt

Pink Dough (20g)

Wet Ingredients (10g) plus a drop of pink coloring.

+

Dry Ingredients:
(8g) flour
(2g) almond flour

Black Dough (20g)

Wet Ingredients (10g)

+

Dry Ingredients:
(6g) flour
(2g) almond flour
(2g) Black cocoa powder

Yellow Dough (160g)

Wet Ingredients (80g)

+

Dry Ingredients:
(56g) flour
(12g) almond flour
(12g) kabocha squash powder

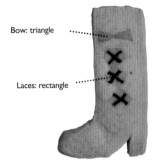

Bow: triangle ·········

Laces: rectangle ·········

1 Form the Shapes (all shapes are 7cm long)

Pink dough (4g):
2 triangles, 0.5 cm (2g each/frozen)

Black dough (8g):
1 sheet, 10cm (chilled)

Yellow dough (152g):
2 sheets, 4cm (11g each/ chilled)
Gap filler (130g/room temp)

>>Instructions: see pages 20-21

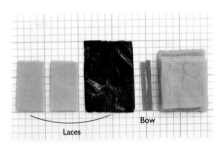

Laces

Bow

2 Make the Laces (1)

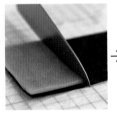

Sandwich half of the black rectangle between the yellow rectangles, slice off the excess black dough and save it for later.

Slice the laces lengthwise into 6 equal portions. Freeze for 5 minutes.

3 Make the Laces (2)

Place a lace on the remainder of the black rectangle as pictured above, slicing off the excess black dough. Adhere this lace to another lace as pictured above, resulting in a cross pattern. Fix the shape as shown above. Repeat two more times. Freeze for 5 minutes.

Use yellow dough to fill the gaps around the laces to make the shape of the boot.

4 Finish the Design

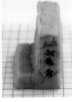

Attach the pink ribbon to the top, then use the rest of your yellow dough to finish the design. Wrap in plastic wrap and adjust the shape. Freeze for 30 minutes.

5 Slice and Shape the Boot

Carefully slice the cookies a little less than ¼" (5 mm) thick, then refine the boot shape by slicing around the heel and toe of each cookie.

6 Bake

Bake in an oven preheated to 275°F (135°C) for 20 to 25 minutes.

Instructions
(makes 12-14 cookies)

1 Combine wet ingredients and separate into 4 portions as shown to the right.

2 Refer to colored dough instructions (right).

3 Combine dry ingredients, sift into each portion of wet ingredients, and combine.

Wet Ingredients (yields 200g)

100g unsalted butter
75g sugar
25g egg (about ½ egg)
2 drops vanilla extract
2 pinches salt

Yellow Dough (40g)

Wet Ingredients (20g)
+
Dry Ingredients:
(14g) flour
(3g) almond flour
(3g) kabotcha squash powder

Brown Dough (40g)

Wet Ingredients (20g)
+
Dry Ingredients:
(14g) flour
(3g) almond flour
(3g) cocoa powder

Blue Dough (50g)

Wet Ingredients (25g) plus a drop of blue coloring.
+
Dry Ingredients:
(22g) flour
(3g) almond flour

Pink Dough (270g)

Wet Ingredients (135g) plus a drop of pink coloring.
+
Dry Ingredients:
(109g) flour
(26g) almond flour

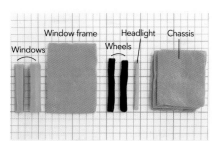

Window: trapezoid

Headlight: square

Wheel: circle

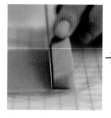

1 Form the Shapes (all shapes are 7cm long)

Window frame   Headlight   Chassis
Windows   Wheels

Yellow dough (2g):
1 square (2g/frozen)

Brown dough (14g):
2 circles (7g each/frozen)

Blue dough (24g):
2 trapezoids, 1.5cm base
(12g each/frozen)

Pink dough (24g):
3 sheets, 8cm (35g each/room temp)
1sheet, 9cm (40g/room temp)

>>Instructions: see pages 20-21

2 Make the Windows

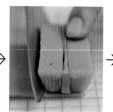
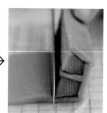

Place a blue trapezoid on the pink rectangle and slice off the excess.

Attach another blue trapezoid to the pink side of the previous shape, then lay the design on a pink rectangle.

Roll the pink dough up around the sides of the window shape. Fix the design, then freeze for 5 minutes.

3 Make the Chassis

Form the chassis by attaching the wheel circles to a pink rectangle. Add a little filler around the wheels to keep them in place. Then add the headlights, fix the shape, and freeze for 10 minutes.

4 Finish the Design

Flip over the chassis and attach the extra pink chassis rectangle to the top to thicken it. Adjust the shape.

If the underside of the window trapezoid is not flat, flatten it before attaching it to the top of the chassis. When finished, wrap in plastic wrap and adjust the shape. Freeze for 20 minutes.

5 Slice and Bake

Carefully slice the cookies a little less than ¼" (5 mm) thick and bake in an oven preheated to 275°F (135°C) for 20 to 25 minutes.

Note: When you cut the cookies, keep the tire-side down. If the shape is damaged in the process, fix it with your fingertips before baking.

Instructions
(makes 12-14 cookies)

1 Combine wet ingredients and separate into 3 portions as shown to the right.

2 Refer to colored dough instructions (right).

3 Combine dry ingredients, sift into each portion of wet ingredients, and combine.

Wet Ingredients (yields 200g)

100g unsalted butter
75g sugar
25g egg (about ½ egg)
2 drops vanilla extract
2 pinches salt

Pink Dough (60g)

Wet Ingredients (30g) plus a drop of pink coloring.
+
Dry Ingredients:
(26g) flour
(4g) almond flour

Brown Dough (60g)

Wet Ingredients (30g)
+
Dry Ingredients:
(22g) flour
(4g) almond flour
(4g) cocoa powder

Plain Dough (280g)

Wet Ingredients (140g)
+
Dry Ingredients:
(119g) flour
(21g) almond flour

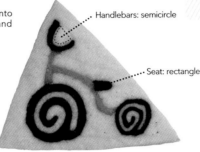

- - Handlebars: semicircle

- - Seat: rectangle

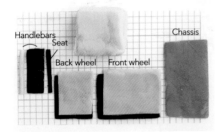

1 Form the Shapes (all shapes are 7cm long)

Pink dough (28g):
1 sheet, 12cm (room temp)

Brown dough (48g):
1 sheet, 0.5cm (2g/frozen)
1 sheet, 10cm (30g/room temp)
1 sheet, 6cm (11g/room temp)
1 sheet, 2.5cm (5g/room temp)

Plain dough (271g):
1 semicircle (4g/frozen)
1 sheet, 9cm (20g/room temp)
1 sheet, 5.5cm (7g/room temp)
gap filler (240 g/room temp)

>>Instructions: see pages 20-21

2 Make the Handlebars

Wrap the brown rectangle (handlebars) around the plain semicircle, discarding any excess brown dough. Freeze for 5 minutes.

3 Make the Wheels

Place the plain rectangle (back wheel) on top of the brown rectangle (back wheel) and roll up. Repeat with the plain and brown rectangles for the large wheel. Freeze for 10 minutes.

4 Attach the Front Wheel

Place the wheel spiral on a sheet of plain dough, then use sticks of gap filler plain dough to fix it in place.

5 Attach the Chassis

1.5cm

Lay a sheet of plain dough over the wheel, then use the pink dough to from the chassis shape above. The vertical portion is a 1.5cm strip of the pink dough.

6 Attach Seat and Tire

Attach the back wheel, cover with plain dough, then attach the seat as shown.

7 Finish the Design

Continue forming the shape with plain dough until you reach the top. Attach the handlebars from step one, then finish the shape with plain dough. When finished, wrap in plastic wrap and adjust the shape. Freeze for 30 minutes.

8 Slice and Fix Shape

Carefully slice the cookies a little less than ¼" (5 mm) thick. Once the cookies are sliced, you can fix the shape by cutting the sides.

9 Bake

Bake in an oven preheated to 275°F (135°C) for 20 to 25 minutes.

Instructions
(makes 12-14 cookies)

1 Combine wet ingredients and separate into 5 portions as shown to the right.

2 Refer to colored dough instructions (right).

3 Combine dry ingredients, sift into each portion of wet ingredients, and combine.

Star: triangle

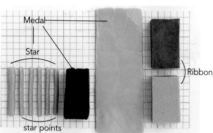

Medal
Star
Ribbon
star points

Wet Ingredients (yields 200g)

100g unsalted butter
75g sugar
25g egg (about ½ egg)
2 drops vanilla extract
2 pinches salt

Yellow Dough (30g)

Wet Ingredients (15g)
+
Dry Ingredients:
  (11g) flour
  (2g) almond flour
  (2g) kabocha squash
    powder

Blue Dough (80g)

Wet Ingredients (40)
plus a drop of blue
coloring.
+
Dry Ingredients:
  (34g) flour
  (6g) almond flour

Black Dough (90g)

Wet Ingredients (45g)
+
Dry Ingredients:
  (33g) flour
  (6g) almond flour
  (4g) black cocoa
    powder
  (2g) cocoa powder

Pink Dough (100g)

Wet Ingredients (50g)
plus a drop of pink
coloring.
+
Dry Ingredients:
  (43g) flour
  (7g) almond flour

Violet Dough (100g)

Wet Ingredients (50g)
+
Dry Ingredients:
  (36g) flour
  (7g) almond flour
  (7g) purple potato
    powder

1 Form the Shapes (all shapes are 7cm long)

Yellow dough (26g):
  1 circle (6g/room temp)
  5 triangles, base 1cm (4g each/frozen)

Blue dough (70g):
  1 sheet, 19cm (room temp)

>>Instructions: see pages 20-21

Black dough (80g):
  gap filler (240 g/room temp)

Pink dough (100g):
  1 rectangle, 4.5cm (chilled)

Violet dough (100g):
  1 rectangle, 4.5cm (chilled)

2 Make the Star

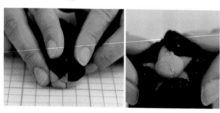

Make the star by attaching the 5 yellow triangles to the outside of the yellow circle. Fill in the gaps with black dough to form the shape. Attaching the triangles is easier if you use a toothpick.

3 Make the Medal

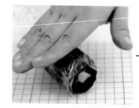

Wrap in plastic wrap and lightly roll to adjust the round shape. Freeze for 10 minutes.

Wrap the blue rectangle around the interior of the medal one time, then discard any excess blue dough. Wrap in plastic wrap and adjust the shape. Freeze for 20 minutes.

4 Make the Ribbon Stripes and Slice

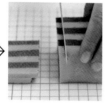

Slice the pink and purple rectangles horizontally lengthwise into 3 portions of equal thickness, then alternate the colors as pictured above. Cover with plastic wrap and press together to adhere stripes. Freeze for 10 minutes.

Carefully slice the cookies (both the ribbon and medal) a little less than ¼" (5 mm) thick.

5 Attach the Ribbon

Slice a curve along the top of the ribbon to fit the curve of the medal and attach.

6 Bake

Bake in an oven preheated to 275°F (135°C) for 20 to 25 minutes.

Play around with the ribbon shapes. Three examples are pictured.

Instructions
(makes 12-14 cookies)

1 Combine wet ingredients and separate into 3 portions as shown to the right.

2 Refer to colored dough instructions (right).

3 Combine dry ingredients, sift into each portion of wet ingredients, and combine.

Wet Ingredients (yields 400g)

200g unsalted butter
150g sugar
50g egg (about 1 egg)
4 drops vanilla extract
4 pinches salt

Plain Dough (100g)

Wet Ingredients (50)
+
Dry Ingredients:
(43g) flour
(7g) almond flour

Black Dough (200g)

Wet Ingredients (100g)
+
Dry Ingredients:
(70g) flour
(15g) almond flour
(10g) black cocoa powder
(5g) cocoa powder

Yellow Dough (500g)

Wet Ingredients (250g)
+
Dry Ingredients:
(176g) flour
(37g) almond flour
(37g) kabocha squash powder

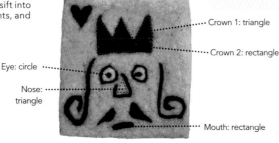

Crown 1: triangle
Crown 2: rectangle
Eye: circle
Nose: triangle
Mouth: rectangle

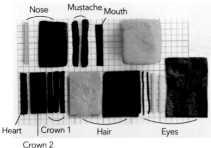

Nose
Mustache Mouth
Heart   Crown 1   Hair   Eyes
Crown 2

1 Form the Shapes (all shapes are 7cm long)

Black dough (91g):
(mustache) 2 triangles (4g each/chilled)
(heart) 1 triangle (6g/chilled)
(crown1) 3 triangles (5g each/frozen)
(crown 2) 1 sheet, 3cm (15g/frozen)
(mouth) 1 sheet, 1cm (3g/frozen)
(eyes) 2 thin sticks (1g each/ frozen)
(hair) 2 sheets, 6cm (11g each/room temp)
(eyes) 1 sheet, 9cm (10g/room temp)
(nose) 1 sheet, 5cm (10g/room temp)

Yellow dough (352g):
(nose) 1 triangle (4g/frozen)
(hair) 2 sheets, 5.5cm
(9g each/room temp)
gap filler (330 g/room temp)

Plain dough (6g):
(eyes) 2 circles (3g each/room temp)

>>Instructions: see pages 20-21

2 Make the Heart

Carve the black triangle (heart) into a heart shape. Freeze for 5 minutes.

3 Make the Eyes

Slice open a plain circle and sandwich a thin black stick between the two halves. Wrap this "eyeball" in a black rectangle, discarding any excess black dough. Repeat for the second eye. Freeze for 5 minutes.

4 Make the Nose

Wrap the yellow triangle in the black rectangle to make the nose outline and slice off any excess black dough. Freeze for 5 minutes.

5 Make the Crown

Place the 3 black triangles (crown) on the black rectangle (crown), filling in the gaps between the triangles with yellow gap filler.

6 Make the Mustache

Form a curve at the tips of the 2 black triangles (moustache) to shape the moustache. Freeze for 5 minutes.

7 Make the Hair

Place one of the yellow rectangles on top of a black rectangle (hair), 3/8" (1 cm) from the edge of the black rectangle. Roll as pictured above. Repeat for the other side of the hair. Freeze for 5 minutes.

8 Finish the Design

Use yellow gap filler to attach the parts made in the previous steps, working up from mouth, mustache, nose eyes, crown, hair, and heart. When finished, wrap in plastic wrap and adjust the shape. Freeze for 30 minutes.

9 Slice and Bake

Carefully slice the cookies a little less than ¼" (5 mm) thick and bake in an oven preheated to 275°F (135°C) for 20 to 25 minutes.

19
Presents
★

>> Instructions: see page 56

21
Candles
★ ★

>> Instructions: see page 58

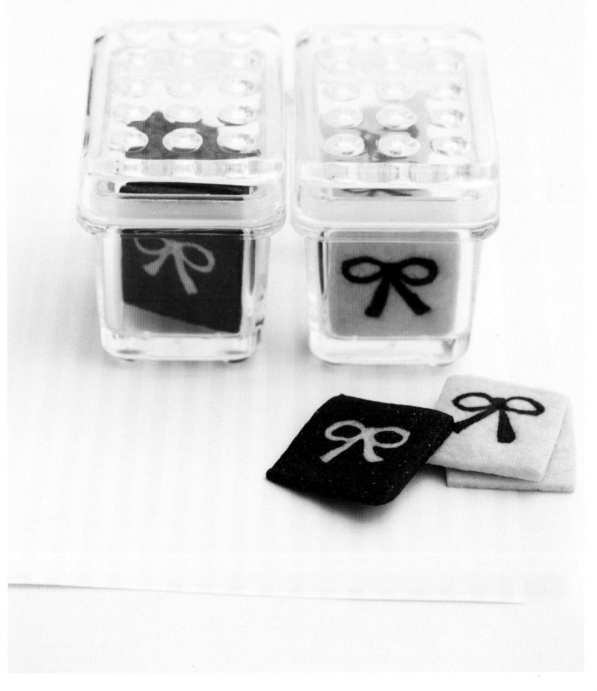

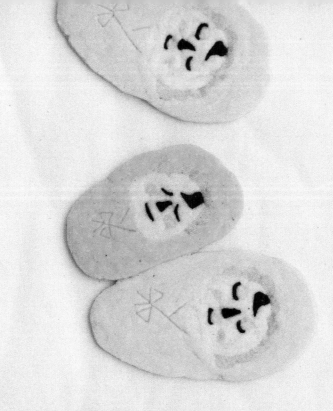

23
Babies
★ ★ ★

>> Instructions: see page 60

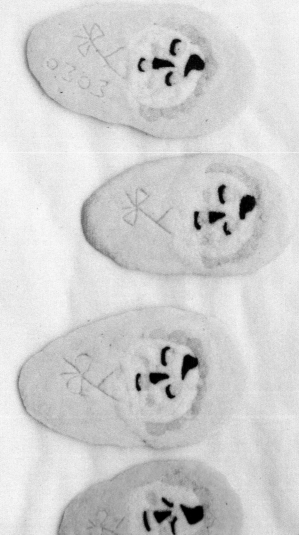

24
Cakes
★ ★

>> Instructions: see page 61

Instructions
(makes 12–14 cookies)

1 Combine wet ingredients and separate into 3 portions as shown to the right.

2 Refer to colored dough instructions (right).

3 Combine dry ingredients, sift into each portion of wet ingredients, and combine.

Wet Ingredients (yields 200g)

100g unsalted butter
75g sugar
25g egg (about ½ egg)
2 drops vanilla extract
2 pinches salt

Ribbon bow: triangle

Pink Dough (80g)

Wet Ingredients (40g) plus a drop of pink coloring.

+

Dry Ingredients:
(34g) flour
(6g) almond flour

Plain Dough (140g)

Wet Ingredients (70g)
+
Dry Ingredients:
(60g) flour
(10g) almond flour

Brown Dough (180g)

Wet Ingredients (90g)
+
Dry Ingredients:
(64g) flour
(13g) almond flour
(13g) cocoa powder

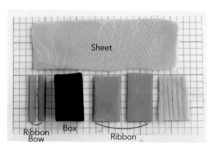

Sheet

Ribbon Bow | Box | Ribbon

1 Form the Shapes (all parts are 7cm long)

Pink dough (62g):
2 sheets, 4cm (25g/chilled)
2 triangles, 1cm base(6g/frozen)

Brown dough (140g):
1 rectangle, 4x4cm (chilled)

Plain dough (120g):
1 sheet, 22 cm(90g/room temp)
gap filler (30g/room temp)

2 Make the Box and Ribbon

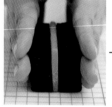

Cut the brown box in half, then sandwich a pink ribbon in the middle.

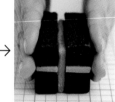

Slice the shape in half perpendicular to the ribbon stripe, then insert another ribbon rectangle as above.

3 Fix the Shape

Use a knife to form straight edges.

4 Attach the Bow

Use plain dough gap filler to attach the two ribbon bows to the top.

5 Finish the Design

Lay a sheet of plain dough on the plastic wrap, and lay step 4 on top. Use the wrap to help roll the plain dough around the design once, then cut off the excess. Use the plastic wrap to fix the final shape, then harden in the freezer for about 30 minutes.

6 Slice and Bake

Carefully slice the cookies a little less than ¼" (5 mm) thick and bake in an oven preheated to 275°F (135°C) for 20 to 25 minutes.

Instructions
(makes 12-14 cookies)

1 Combine wet ingredients and separate into 4 portions as shown to the right.

2 Refer to colored dough instructions (right).

3 Combine dry ingredients, sift into each portion of wet ingredients, and combine.

Wet Ingredients (yields 200g)

100g unsalted butter
75g sugar
25g egg (about ½ egg)
2 drops vanilla extract
2 pinches salt

Dark Blue Dough (60g)

Wet Ingredients (30) plus a drop of blue coloring.

+

Dry Ingredients:
(25g) flour
(5g) almond flour

Light Blue Dough (80g)

Wet Ingredients (30) plus a drop of blue coloring.

+

Dry Ingredients:
(25g) flour
(5g) almond flour

Different blues can be made by varying the amount of food coloring in the recipe.

Yellow Dough (80g)

Wet Ingredients (40g)

+

Dry Ingredients:
(28g) flour
(6g) almond flour
(6g) kabocha squash powder

Pink Dough (200g)

Wet Ingredients (100g) plus a drop of pink coloring.

+

Dry Ingredients:
(85g) flour
(15g) almond flour

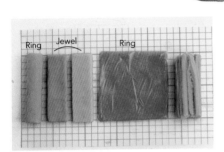

Ring (circle) ··········

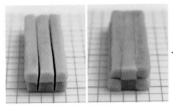

Ring | Jewel | Ring

1 Form the Shapes (all parts are 10cm long)

Dark blue dough (40g):
1 sheet, 3cm (chilled)
Light blue dough (40g):
1 sheet, 3cm sheet (chilled)
Yellow dough (60g):
1 sheet, 10cm (room temp)

Pink dough (165g):
1 circle (55 g / frozen)
gap filler (110g/ room temp)

≫Instructions pp20,21

2 Make the Gemstone

Cut the dark and light blue sheets into three portions, then alternate as shown. Use plastic wrap to fix the shape.

Slice into a diamond shape, then freeze for 5 minutes.

3 Make the Ring

place the yellow sheet onto plastic wrap, then roll it around the pink circle. Slice off any excess yellow dough.

Roll over the board to make an even shape.

4 Attach the Ring

Use pink gap filler to attach the jewel to the ring. Freeze for 5 minutes.

5 Finish the Design

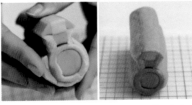

Use the remaining pink gap filler to finish the shape. cover in plastic wrap, fix the shape, then freeze for 20 mintues.

6 Remove the Center

Slice the cookies, then use a knife to remove the center from the ring.

7 Slice and Bake

Bake in an oven preheated to 275°F (135°C) for 20 to 25 minutes.

Instructions
(Number of cookies varies with design)

1 Combine wet ingredients and separate into 5 portions as shown to the right.

2 Refer to colored dough instructions (right).

3 Combine dry ingredients, sift into each portion of wet ingredients, and combine.

Wet Ingredients (yields 200g)

100g unsalted butter
75g sugar
25g egg (about ½ egg)
2 drops vanilla extract
2 pinches salt

Pink Dough (150g)

Wet Ingredients (25g) plus a drop of pink coloring.

+

Dry Ingredients:
(21g) flour
(4g) almond flour

Blue Dough (50g)

Wet Ingredients (25g) plus a drop of blue coloring.

+

Dry Ingredients:
(21g) flour
(4g) almond flour

Violet Dough (80g)

Wet Ingredients (40g)

+

Dry Ingredients:
(28g) flour
(6g) almond flour
(6g) purple potato powder

Plain Dough (80g)

Wet Ingredients (40g)

+

Dry Ingredients:
(34g) flour
(6g) almond flour

Black Dough (140g)

Wet Ingredients (70g)

+

Dry Ingredients:
(50g) flour
(10g) almond flour
(7g) black cocoa powder
(3g) cocoa powder

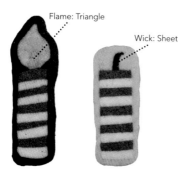

Flame: Triangle
Wick: Sheet

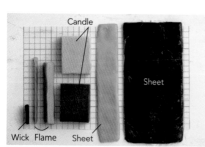

Candle
Sheet
Wick Flame Sheet

1 Form the Shapes (all parts are different lengths)

Pink dough (45g):
Flame:10cm long triangle (45g/room temp)

Blue dough (46g):
10cm long triangle (6g/frozen)
1 sheet, 3x20cm (40g/room temp)

Violet dough (80g):
Candle: 6.5x5cm rectangle (chilled)

Plain dough (80g):
1 rectangle, 6.5x5cm (chilled)

Black dough (133g):
Wick: 3x1cm sheet (3g/frozen)
1 sheet, 10x20cm (10g/room temp)
gap filler (20g/room temp)

2 Make the Flame

Make a cut in the pink flame, then insert the blue flame into the cut.

Use your fingers to shape the pink portion into a flame shape, then freeze for 10 miuntes.

3 Make the Stripes for the Candle

3.5cm 3cm

Slice the plain and purple candle portions into 10 pieces, then alternate them to form stripes. Use plastice wrap to fully adhere them into one shape.

You will have two 6.5cm striped rectangles. Divide one into 3.5cm and 3cm portions as shown, then attach the 3.5cm portion to the full 6.5 cm rectangle to form a 10cm rectangle and a 3cm rectangle

4 Attach the Flame

Use black gap filler to attach the flame to the 10cm rectangle, then freeze for 10 minutes.

Attach the Wick

Use a little blue dough to attach the black wick to the 3cm rectangle, then freeze for 5 minutes.

5 Finish the Design

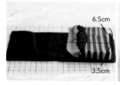

6.5cm
3.5cm

Lay the black sheet on plastic wrap and then place the 10cm candle with flame on it. Wrap once in the black sheet, then trim excess. Freeze for 30 minutes.

Use the blue dough to do the same thing to the wick version.

6 Slice and Bake

Bake in an oven preheated to 275°F (135°C) for 20 to 25 minutes.

Instructions
(makes 12–14 cookies)

1 Combine wet ingredients and separate into 2 portions as shown to the right.

2 Refer to colored dough instructions (right).

3 Combine dry ingredients, sift into each portion of wet ingredients, and combine.

Wet Ingredients (yields 200g)

100g unsalted butter
75g sugar
25g egg (about ½ egg)
2 drops vanilla extract
2 pinches salt

Black Dough (100g)

Wet Ingredients (50g)
+
Dry Ingredients:
(36g) flour
(7g) almond flour
(5g) black cocoa powder
(2g) cocoa powder

Pink Dough (300g)

Wet Ingredients (150g)
plus a drop of pink coloring.
+
Dry Ingredients:
(128g) flour
(22g) almond flour

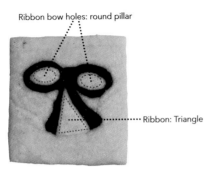

Ribbon bow holes: round pillar

Ribbon: Triangle

SWITCH THE COLORS!

Pink Dough (100g)

Wet Ingredients (50g)
plus a drop of pink coloring.
+
Dry Ingredients:
(43g) flour
(7g) almond flour

Black Dough (300g)

Wet Ingredients (150g)
+
Dry Ingredients:
(106g) flour
(22g) almond flour
(15g) black cocoa powder
(7g) cocoa powder

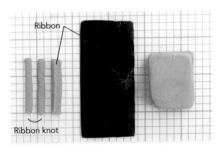

Ribbon

Ribbon knot

1 Form the Shapes (all parts are 7cm long)

Black dough (30g):
1 sheet, 14cm (room temp)

Pink dough:
2 ovals (4g each / frozen)
1 triangle, base 1cm (8g / frozen)
gap filler (210g / room temp)

2 Make the Ribbon Loops

Use the black sheet to wrap the pink circles, cutting off any excess. Freeze for 5 mintues.

3 Make the Ribbon

Use the remaining black sheet to wrap two sides of the pink triangle, cutting off any excess. Fix the shape with your fingers, and freeze for 5 minutes.

4 Attach the Loops

Press the ribbon bows on to a sheet of pink gap filler, then lay a small strip of black dough between them to fill out the design.

5 Finish the Design

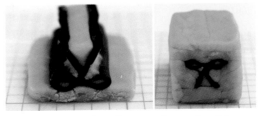

Attach the triangle shape from step three, using pink gap filler. Continue adding pink dough until the design is complete. Use plastic wrap to fix the shape, then freeze for 30 mintues.

6 Slice and Bake

Bake in an oven preheated to 275°F (135°C) for 20 to 25 minutes.

23 Babies

Instructions
(makes 12–14 cookies)

1 Combine wet ingredients and separate into 4 portions as shown to the right.

2 Refer to colored dough instructions (right).

3 Combine dry ingredients, sift into each portion of wet ingredients, and combine.

Wet Ingredients (yields 200g)

100g unsalted butter
75g sugar
25g egg (about ½ egg)
2 drops vanilla extract
2 pinches salt

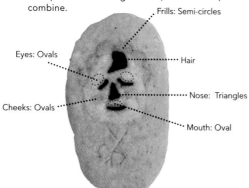

- Frills: Semi-circles
- Eyes: Ovals
- Hair
- Nose: Triangles
- Cheeks: Ovals
- Mouth: Oval

Brown Dough (40g)

Wet Ingredients (20g)
+
Dry Ingredients:
(14g) flour
(3g) almond flour
(3g) cocoa powder

Pink Dough (40g)

Wet Ingredients (20g)
plus a drop of pink coloring.
+
Dry Ingredients:
(17g) flour
(3g) almond flour

Plain Dough (80g)

Wet Ingredients (40g)
+
Dry Ingredients:
(34g) flour
(6g) almond flour

Green Dough (240g)

Wet Ingredients (120g)
plus a drop of green coloring.
+
Dry Ingredients:
(105g) flour
(15g) almond flour

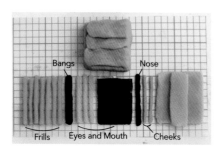

Bangs, Nose, Frills, Eyes and Mouth, Cheeks

1 Form the Shapes (all parts are 7cm long)

Brown dough (11g):
1 triangle (3g/frozen)
1 stick (2g/frozen)
1 sheet, 5cm (6g/room temp)

Pink dough (16–20g):
6–8 semi-circles (2g each/frozen)
2 ovals (2g each/frozen)

Plain dough (66g):
3 ovals (2g each/frozen)
gap filler (60g/room temp)

Green dough (220g):
gap filler (room temp)

2 Make the Eyes and Mouth

Place the plain dough ovals on the brown dough sheet, press together, and slice off excess to form the eyes and mouth.

3 Make the Chin

Use the plain gap filler to make a 2cm strip, then attach the mouth from step 2.

4 Make the Face

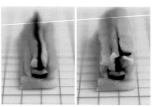

Use your plain dough filler to work up the face, attaching the brown nose, then pink cheeks, then the two eyes.

5 Attach the Hair

Use a little plain dough filler to attach the baby's hair. Use plastic wrap to fix the overall shape.

6 Attach the Frills

Add the pink frills to the top, then freeze for 10 minutes.

7 Finish the Design

Cover the whole design in green gap filler as shown. Use plastic wrap to fix the shape, and then freeze for 30 minutes.

8 Draw the Clothes

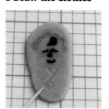

After slicing, use a toothpick to draw a clothing pattern.

9 Slice and Bake

Bake in an oven preheated to 275°F (135°C) for 20 to 25 minutes.

Instructions
(makes 12–14 cookies)

1 Combine wet ingredients and separate into 5 portions as shown to the right.

2 Refer to colored dough instructions (right).

3 Combine dry ingredients, sift into each portion of wet ingredients, and combine.

Wet Ingredients (yields 200g)

100g unsalted butter
75g sugar
25g egg (about ½ egg)
2 drops vanilla extract
2 pinches salt

Black Dough (20g)

Wet Ingredients (10g)
+
Dry Ingredients:
(6g) flour
(2g) almond flour
(2g) black cocoa powder

Green Dough (20g)

Wet Ingredients (10g) plus a drop of green coloring.
+
Dry Ingredients:
(8g) flour
(2g) almond flour

Dark Pink Dough (10g)

Wet Ingredients (5g) plus a drop of pink coloring.
+
Dry Ingredients:
(8g) flour
(2g) almond flour

Light Pink Dough (30g)

Wet Ingredients (15g) plus a drop of pink coloring.
+
Dry Ingredients:
(13g) flour
(2g) almond flour

Plain Dough (310g)

Wet Ingredients (155g)
+
Dry Ingredients:
(132g) flour
(23g) almond flour

Different pinks can be made by varying the amount of food coloring in the recipe.

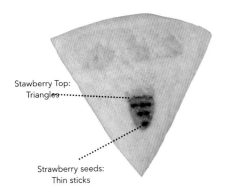

Stawberry Top:
Triangles

Strawberry seeds:
Thin sticks

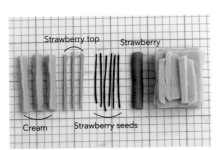

Strawberry top
Strawberry
Cream
Strawberry seeds

1 Form the Shapes (all parts are 7cm long)

Black dough (2g):
6 very thin sticks (very thin/frozen)

Green dough (3g):
3 triangles (1g each/frozen)

Dark pink dough (14g):
1 cm base triangle (room temp)

Light pink dough (24g):
3 triangles (8g each/chilled)

Plain dough (310g):
gap filler (room temp)

2 Make the Strawberry

Cut the dark pink triangle into 4 parts horizontally, then add the 6 black sticks and reform the triangle. Fix the shape, add the green top, and freeze for 5 minutes.

3 Make the Cream

Pinch the light pink triangles so that they resemble dollops of cream. Freeze for 5 minutes.

4 Make Strawberry

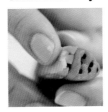

Fill the gaps around the strawberry top with plain gap filler and freeze for 5 minutes.

5 Attach the Cream

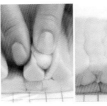

Attach the three dollops of cream to a plain sheet of gap filler. Fill the gaps between them, then flip the design over.

6 Finish the Design

Use the remaining plain gap filler to attach the strawberry, and then to fill out the rest of the design. Use plastic wrap to fix the shape, then freeze for 30 minutes.

7 Slice to Desired Shape

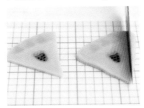

Slice the cookies, then use a knife to fix the shape.

8 Bake

Bake in an oven preheated to 275°F (135°C) for 20 to 25 minutes.

2
Langues de Chat

Here we make four different shapes from a plain dough, and using 7 colored doughs you may freely draw whatever patterns you choose.
If you have leftover dough, use your imagination to make whatever you want!

25
Cigarette style
★
>> Instructions: see page 73

26
Spirals
★
>> Instructions: see page 73

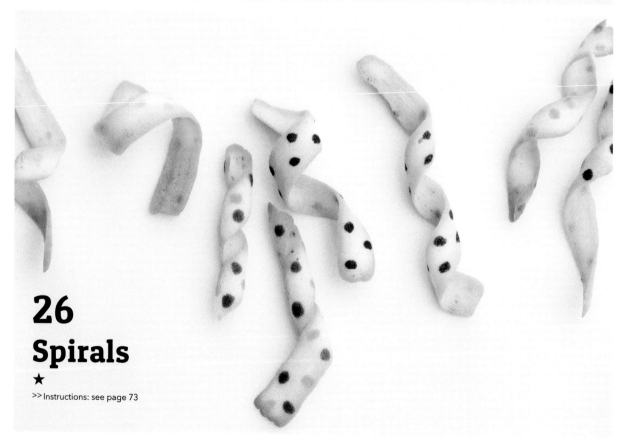

27
Cup style
★
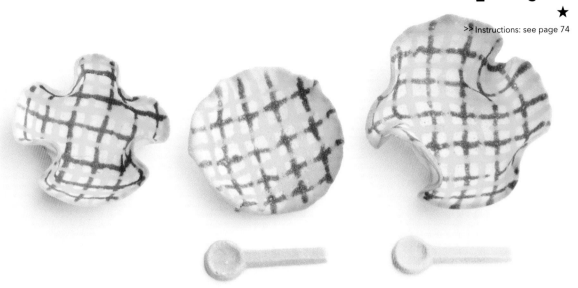

>> Instructions: see page 74

28
Cone style
★★
>> Instructions: see page 74

29
Patterns
★
>> Instructions: see page 75

30
Words
★★
>> Instructions: see page 75

HOW TO MAKE THE DOUGH

The basic Langue de Chat dough is made by sifting flour and almond powder into a base of butter, sugar, eggs, and cream. For the remainder of this book this dough will be called "Plain Dough".

HERE WE EXPLAIN THE BASIC PROCESS FOR MAKING PLAIN AND COLORED LANGUE DE CHAT DOUGHS. ALL THE RECIPES TO FOLLOW MAKE USE OF THE DOUGHS EXPLAINED IN THIS SECTION, SO MAKE SURE YOU HAVE MASTERED THESE DOUGHS BEFORE MOVING ON.

Ingredients (yields 220g)

50g unsalted butter
50g sugar
30g (about 1) egg white
30g heavy cream
30g almond powder
30g flour
2 drops vanilla extract
Pinch of salt

Instructions

1 Put softened (room temperature) butter into bowl and work it with a rubber spatula until it reaches a cream-like consistency.

2 Separate the sugar into two equal portions and add them to the butter, one after the other, working the mixture constantly until it turns white and fluffy.

3 Separate the eggs (also room temperature) into three equal portions and add them to the mixture, one after the other, until the mix comes together.

4 Slowly add (mixing all the while) the heavy cream to the mixture. Finally, add the vanilla extract and salt.

5 Sift in the almond powder all at once, then stir.

6 Sift in the flour all at once, then stir.

HOW TO MAKE COLORED DOUGHS

Food coloring is used to make the pink, blue, green, yellow, and violet doughs, while powders are used for the black and brown doughs. All in all you end up with 7 different colors.

**Food Coloring
AND
Natural Powders**

Instructions

1 Divide the plain dough into the number of colors you will need, and to each portion at food coloring or powders until the desired color is achieved. Mix with a rubber spatula.

2 Add the mixture into a piping bag, and cut a 1mm hole at the point. The size of the hole may be adjusted depending on the desired effect.

Food Coloring

Pink dough   Yellow dough
Green dough   Violet dough
Blue dough

Natural Powders

Black dough (black cocoa powder)
Brown dough (cocoa powder)

ONCE YOU'VE GOT THE DOUGH MADE...

Once you have your dough prepared, flip through the recipes, find one you'd like to emulate, and get drawing! If the dough gets too stiff it will crack, so work quickly, but take care not to burn yourself!

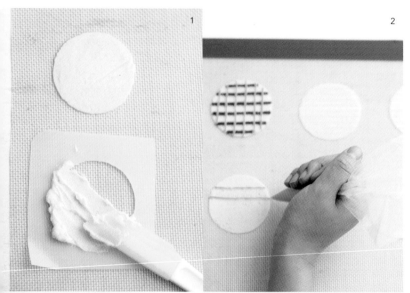

Instructions

Make the desired shape

1 Spread plain dough onto an baking sheet in whatever shape you desire, but keep them about 2mm thick. The more even the dough, the better.

Draw a pattern

2 Using colored doughs, draw a pattern onto the plain dough. When the cookies are baked, the dough will spread a little bit, so keep that in mind when you are drawing.

Bake

3 Bake in an oven pre-heated to 320°F (160°C), until the edges of the cookies brown and they spring back when poked. While the cookies are still hot, remove them from the baking sheet with a pallet knife and quickly form them into the desired shape (careful not to burn yourself!). As the cookies cool they will become brittle, so work quickly. If they cool too quickly, they can be warmed in the oven until they become pliable again.

Storage

4 Langue de Chat turn stale relatively quickly, so be sure to store them in tupperware with a desiccant. Wait for them to cool completely before you close the tupperware.

25
Cigarette style

Makes 25-30 cookies
Plain dough 160g
2 Colored doughs 30g each

Instructions

1 Form a circle

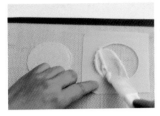

Using a rubber spatula, spread the dough into 6cm circles.

*This is much easier with a circular stencil

→

Use a scraper to level out the dough

2 Draw a pattern

Using a piping bag, draw a pattern onto the plain dough with your colored dough

3 Roll

After baking for 5 - 7 minutes in a 320°F (160°C) oven, roll the still-warm circles around a thick chopstick.

26
Spirals

Makes 25-30 cookies
Plain dough 160g
2 Colored Doughs 30g each

Instructions

1 Draw sticks

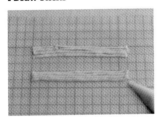

Using a piping bag, draw sticks of dough about 11 cm long.

*This is much easier with a lined cutting board under the baking sheet

2 Draw a pattern

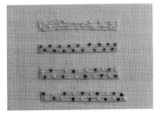

Using colored doughs in piping bags, draw a pattern onto the plain dough

3 Roll

After baking for 5 - 7 minutes in a 320°F (160°C) oven, roll the still warm sticks around a thick chopstick.

27
Cup style

Makes 7-8 cookies
Plain dough 160g
2 Colored doughs 30g each

Instructions

1 Form a circle

Using a rubber spatula, spread the dough into 12cm circles.

*This is much easier with a circular stencil.

→

Use a spatula to level out the dough.

2 Draw a pattern

Using colored doughs in piping bags, draw a pattern onto the plain dough.

3 Mold into a cup

After baking for 7 - 8 minutes in a 320°F (160°C) oven, place the circle into a 10cm bowl and frill the edges.

Using the outside of the bowl, a larger shape can be made, If the dough is too hot to work with, use some napkins to form the cookie around the exterior of the bowl.

28
Cone style

Makes 7-8 cookies
Plain dough 160g
2 Colored doughs 30g each

Instructions

1 Make a fan-shape

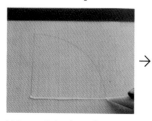

→

Using a piping bag, draw a fan shape with plain dough, aiming for about 11 cm.

*This is easier if you place the baking sheet over a pattern to trace.

Use a spatula to level out the dough

2 Draw a pattern

Using colored doughs in piping bags, draw a pattern onto the plain dough

3 Roll

After baking for 5 - 7 minutes in a 320°F (160°C) oven, roll the still warm cookies around a cone-shaped mold.

*The mold can be made out of anything from construction paper to styrofoam. The molds are best wrapped in aluminum foil before use.

29
Patterns

Ingredients
Plain dough
Colored dough

Draw the Patterns

 →

Using dough in a piping bag, draw the desired pattern directly onto the baking sheet.

Bake in an oven preheated to 320°F (160°C) for 7 to 10 minutes. The amount of time necessary will vary with the size of the cookie, but if they spring back when pressed with a fingertip, they are done.

MEMO

The cookies will spread a little when baking. If you make the shapes close to one another, they will come together in the oven and create fun shapes.

30
Words

Ingredients
Colored dough

1 Draw a Shape You Like

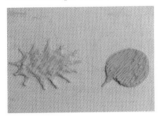

Draw a fun shape using a piping bag filled with colored dough. Note: Make sure that the dough is all the same thickness.

2 Write the Words

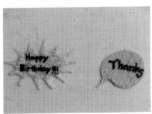

Again, using a piping bag, write out the desired message onto the shape you have drawn. Bake in an oven preheated to 320°F (160°C) for 7 to 10 minutes.

MEMO

The dough will expand when baking, so if you are making a particularly complicated shape or message, consider making the dough thinner than normal.

31
Pictures

Ingredients
Plain dough
Colored dough

1 Draw a Picture

Draw a fun shape using a piping bag filled with colored dough. Note: Make sure that the dough is all the same thickness.

2 Draw the Patterns

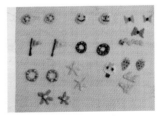

Using a piping bag, draw some patterns onto the pictures you have drawn. Bake in an oven preheated to 320°F (160°C) for 7 to 10 minutes.

MEMO

When you are only baking a small amount of dough, the fan in the oven may cause the baking sheet to blow around inside the oven. This can be prevented by using a little dough to "glue" the baking sheet to the baking tray, or by using metal spoons to weigh down the sheet.

AFTERWORD

→→————————————→

EVER SINCE I WAS YOUNG, I LOVED TO WATCH PEOPLE MAKE THINGS.

When I was a child, right before I left for school in the morning, there was a ten-minute cooking program on the television, and watching it was the most fun I had all day.

I remember that after school I would run home and try to recreate the dish that I'd seen that morning. Kids sure are motivated! But I was too young to cook, so I'd recreate the dishes I'd seen with construction paper and tissues.

I'd do the best I could with what I had, and when my projects didn't come out just right, I'd laugh and enjoy them for what they were. I don't think I've changed much in that regard.

When I was a child, I'd wonder if I could really recreate what I'd seen. I'd try all sorts of things, and my hands were always rushing here and there. I'd get excited and giggle and it was always fun. Baking these sweets engenders those same feelings in me still.

In the end it was a ribbon-shaped cookie. A lot of people liked it, and it was picked up by various outlets before eventually catching the eye of Mr. Hoshino at the Kawade Publishing company. That was how this book came to be.

I didn't understand much about the entire photographing process, and probably was just in everyone's hair, but the stylist and cameraman and designer and editors, also my family, friends, and students, everyone came together to help make this book a reality. I'm so happy I don't know what to say. Thank you all very much.

I hope that your cookies will bring joy to others!